Great Masjids of My African Homeland

A Coloring Book of Africa's Great Mosques

Table of Contents

Introduction   5

Masjid of the Companions, Abbysinnia (modern-day Eritrea, Africa)   6

The Grand Mosque of Timbo   8

The Mosque of Bode   10

The Mosque of Kobilo   12

The Mosque of Guede   14

The Mosque of Doumga   16

Sidi Yahya Mosque   18

Jingereber Mosque   20

Sankore Mosque   22

Central Mosque of Illorin   24

The Great Mosque of Kilwa   26

Masjid of al-Hajj Umar Tall   28

The Great Mosque of Touba   30

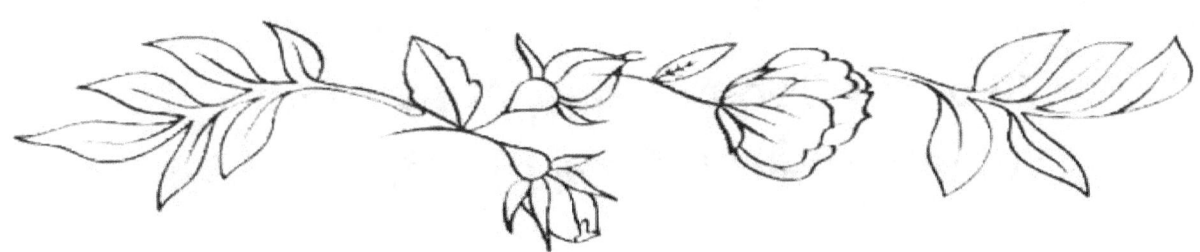

As Salaamu Alaikum

Most of the events in the Quran take place in Africa. One scholar has called the Qur'an a great source for learning of the history of Africa. The first Hijira takes place in Africa. The first monarch to accept Islam occurs in Africa. In fact, Africa is the first place in the world where Muslims have true religious freedom, and are able to practice their faith without any persecution. This coloring book celebrates one segment of the many Islamic jewels on the African continent – the African Masjids. The histories of both Islam and Africa are uniquely intertwined and inextricably linked. Thus, even for the non-Muslim, this coloring book is quite useful as it delves into the rich history of the world's second largest continent. A focus on African Masjids, is an interesting way to engage children with both the history of our African forebears, and of the beautiful religion of Islam. The early Masjids in West Africa sought to resemble the model constructed and used by Prophet Muhammad (Peace Be Upon Him). This early model was simple, yet elegant and serene. The Masjids of Muslims in West Africa during the precolonial period, were thus also known for their simplicity, elegance, and serenity – but with an African twist. The terrain in West Africa and the Arabian desert are quite different from one another. Thus, in constructing their own Masjids, West Africans utilized the tools and resources within the environment provided them by Allah.

As educators, it's important for us to support students in building self-confidence in their cultural identities, as well as awareness and appreciation for diversity. This book is tool in that direction. We invite you to open-up the world of worship to the one true God, which has been practiced by your ancestors for over 1000 years (over 1400 years in some places). There are over 500 million Muslims in Africa today. This makes Africa the only continent in the world where Muslims constitute a majority of the population. In fact, there are more Muslims in just Sub-Saharan Africa than in the entire Middle East region. Recent scholarship has shown that almost 50% of Africans trafficked in the Trans-Saharan Slave cartel were Muslims. This makes Muslims the largest contingent of Africans sent to the Americas. Thus, most African Americans, Afro-Brazilians, present-day Jamaicans, Haitians, and other Black populations of the African Diaspora throughout the Americas, are descendants of African Muslims. This coloring book connects us spiritually to our pious ancestors, and also enhances our own understanding of who we are and where we come from.

We look forward to embarking on this journey of discovery and adventure with you.

Wassalam

Masjid of the Companions, Abbysinnia (modern-day Eritrea, Africa)

The Masjid of the Companions is the Africa's first Masjid, and one of the earliest Masjids in the world. It is the first Masjid ever completed without the Holy Prophet, as well as the first Masjid constructed outside of Arabia. When the early Muslims were being persecuted in Mecca for worshipping Allah instead of the many idols of the society, Prophet Muhammad sought protection from the king of Abbysinnia. Prophet Muhammad sent many of his Companions to Abbysinnia to live under the king's protection until it was safe for them to return. While, the Companions created the Masjid of the Companions, and they were free to worship Allah without any worry of harm coming their way. Because of this, many scholars say that Abbysinnia is the first place on Earth where freedom of religion was both established and exercised.

The Grand Mosque of Timbo

One of the earliest and most important Masjids in West Africa, is the Grand Mosque of Timbo at Futa Jallon (located in present-day Guinea). The Masjid was inaugurated in the mid-17th century with the successful Islamic revolution of Futa Jallon led by the Fulani.. The Fulani then created the Fulbe Confederacy which consisted of nine principal provinces, a group of elders, and an Almamy to serve as supreme leader. Karamoka Alpha was elected as the first Al-mamy of Futa Jallon, because of his calm demeanor, knowledge and piety, as well as his capacity to forgive. He was given a sword and nine turbans to represent his duty to protect Islam and his people within each of the nine provinces. It's also here in Futa Jallon, where the Qur'an was first translated into an African language (Fulfide, the language of the Fulani) by Karamoka Alpha. Under his leadership, the Masjid in Timbo would be reconstructed, and it would become the Grand Masjid due to its location in the hometown of Karamoka Alpha, and in the seat of the province of the Almamies. The roof of this Masjid was made with bamboo rafters, and was not allowed to touch the down during its construction. The ladder leads to a raised platform in the Masjid.

The Mosque of Bode

The Mosque of Bode, Futa Toro was constructed under the direction of Suleyman Baal between 1760 and 1770 (Bourdier, 1993). Suleyman Baal was the second Almamy of Futa Toro, and the cousin of it's first Almamy Karamoka Ba. He was a great military commander under the leadership of his cousin, and was able to help successfully install Islam as the dominant religion in the area. Under Suleyman Baal, Islam flourished in Futa Toro, and the enslavement of Muslims was put to a drastic halt.

ALLAHU AKBAR

The Mosque of Kobilo

The mosque of Kobilo in Futa Toro, is said to be one of the few remaining mosques originally built by the great Almaamy Abdul Kader Kan. Almaamy Abdul Kader Kan became leader of Futa Toro after Suleyman Baal in 1776. As leader of Futa Toro, Almaamy Abdul Kader Kan is said to have constructed a mosque in each village under his control throughout the late 1770s. Always the Islamic teacher, he sought to encourage both literacy and Islamic learning. Building so many mosques in such a short time span is a massive undertaking, and a great demonstration of how devout our African ancestors were within the Islamic tradition. He also stopped the French from buying and enslaving innocent Africans from along the Senegal River. His efforts were cited by the great anti-slavery champion, Lord William Wilberforce in the Parliament of Great Britain.

AL-KHAALIQ
THE CREATOR

The Mosque of Guede

Mosque of Guede, Futa Toro. This mosque, considered the oldest in Toro province, was supposedly first built around the 1670s by the chief of Toro and reconstructed by Abdul Kader Kan in 1776, and by Al-Hajj Umar in the 1850s. It underwent several renovations before its last reconstruction in 1942. The massive tapering pillars give the mosque its Sudanese character.

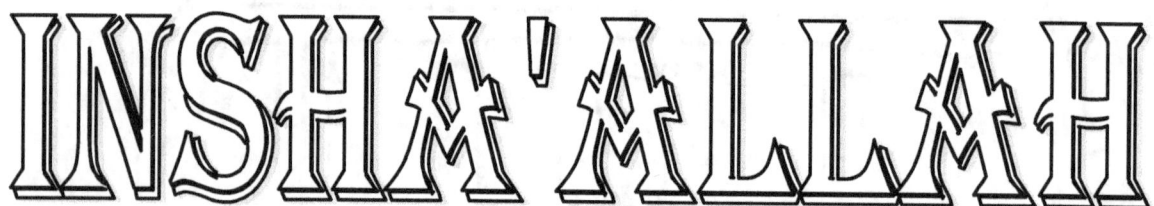

The Mosque of Doumga

Mosque of Doumga Ouro Thierno, Futa Toro. Originally built by Al-mamy Abdul Kader Kan in the late 1800s, the adobe mosque was reconstructed in 1930.

Sidi Yahya Mosque

Sidi Yahya Mosque is one of the three major Masjids of Timbuktu, in present-day Mali. It was constructed in the 15th century by the governor of Timbuktu in honor of the revered Sidi Yahya al-Tadalisi. Sidi Yahya was the Imam of Timbuktu, and he would hold classes at this mosque. Sidi Yahya was exceptional because he was taught by an exceptional leader, the great Shaykh Modibo al-Kabori. (Gomez, 2018).

Jingereber Mosque

Jingereber Mosque is another Mosque located in the famed city of Timbuktu. As Timbuktu is known internationally as the "City of Scholars," it is because of its institutions of learning that it has this unique moniker. Jingereber is one of these great centers of learning, and Jingereber Mosque means the "Great Mosque" in the Songhay language. It was originally built by the legendary Mansa Musa, on his way back from completing his famous pilgrimage in Mecca. As you may have already heard, Mansa Musa was not only the great king of the Malian Empire, but he is also the richest man in world history. Jingereber Mosque was historically the congregational mosque in Timbuktu. This means that it was here where the people, including all the notable and leading citizens, would gather for Friday prayers (Jummah).

As Salaam

Sankore Mosque

Sankore Mosque is perhaps the most famous of the three great Mosques of Timbuktu. Of all these three Mosques, it is Sankore Mosque where multitudes of scholars and students would gather, and take Islamic learning and erudition to higher levels. Students from all over Africa and the Muslim world, would flock to Sankore Mosque to learning the higher echelons of Islamic sciences at the feet of the most learned scholars in all the Muslim world. Disciplines such as the Qur'an, Hadith, Tafsir, Law, etc., were all taught here. Students could also study Logic, Arabic Grammar, Rhetoric, Astronomy, and a host of other subjects as well. Important books would also be taught to students, and after successfully completing the book, instructors would issue them a "jiyza," or license of their own to teach the book they'd just mastered.

Alhamdullilah

23

Central Mosque of Illorin

The Central Mosque of Illorin was built in the late 1970s and is the second largest mosque in Nigeria. The Mosque is a boasts a stunning array of architectural jewels, and designers from over 16 different countries helped to complete it construction. Illorin is a large state in Nigeria and with a large Yoruba population. After the Islamic revolution in the late 18th century, it became one of several new Emirates of the Sokoto Caliphate. The Central Mosque is strategically located in the Northern part of the city, and serves as a meeting place for many different Muslim communities. Illorin itself is a central hub for Northerns seeking to do business in the South, and for Southerners seeking to do business in the North. The presence of the Mosque is one of the elements that allow this collaboration and coordination to function smoothly. Although Illorin is a major Yoruba state, it also has large populations of Fulani, Hausa, Nupe, and other ethnic groups. Despite their ethnic backgrounds, however, Islam serves as their main common denominator. One of the beautiful facts about the Mosque, is that it takes its architectural design from many different cultural, ethnic, and Islamic traditions.

The Great Mosque of Kilwa

This masjid is one of the oldest Masjids in East Africa. It's located on a Tanzanian island just off of Africa's Swahili coast, and was built around the 9th century. The mosque served as the focal point for the area's local Muslim community, and also as one of the primary mosques for seafarers and other travelers moving through the coast. In fact, one of the world's greatest travelers, Ibn Battuta, stopped at the Great Mosque of Kilwa during one of his journeys along the Swahili coast. Battuta called the entire Kilwa area one of the most beautiful places on earth. This mosque boasts several architectural highlights. Its beautiful and massive dome was the largest dome in East Africa until the 19th century. The mosque is also one of the first mosques constructed without a courtyard.

Masjid of al-Hajj Umar Tall

Of all the construction erected during the reign of Sheikh al-Hajj Umar Tall, this masjid in Dinguiraye, Guinea is one of the only remaining structures still standing today. During the 19th century, Sheikh al-Hajj Umar Tall revolted against the ruling powers and called on them to live more faithfully to Islam. It was here in the city of Dinguiraye that al-Hajj Umar Tall would set-up his base of operations and organize/train his own army. At the height of his reign, Tall conquered over 4 independent states, and thus created one of the largest states in Africa. He also took the education of his people very seriously. For instance, he created many mosques, schools, and commanded the most learned among his people to instruct those with little academic training. Sheikh Umar Tall created masjids in every town under his dominion. Today, this masjid is still in use as a primary religious center for the community, and as a haven for those seeking to benefit from its baraka.

The Great Mosque of Touba

The Great Mosque of Touba was founded originally in 1887 by Sheikh Ahmadou Bamba, but was completed in 1963. Today, the Great Mosque of Touba is the largest masjid in West Africa, and one of the great wonders of the entire Islamic world. The mosque is the largest building in Touba and has a capacity of over 7,000 people. Touba is also the home of the Mouride Brotherhood, which was founded by Sheikh Ahmadou Bamba in 1884. The Mouride Brotherhood has branches all over the world (including in the U.S., Canada, Europe, etc.) and is the only Sufi Order with a Black founder. Due to the dedication of the Mourides, and with the example and inspiration of one of Bamba's most important followers, Sheikh Ibrahima Fall, Touba has grown to become Senegal's second largest city. Besides the Great Mosque, it also houses an Islamic University and a world-class public library. Each year, over 3 million pilgrims make the journey to Touba to celebrate the annual festival Grand Magal of Touba).

AL-QADIR